Coming Back from Broken:
A Young Widow's Journey

Coming Back from Broken:
A Young Widow's Journey

Stacie Baker

Stacie Baker
2019

First Printing: 2019

ISBN 978-0-359-73682-9

Stacie Baker
PO Box 14307
Springfield, MO 65814

www.justinsrace.wordpress.com

Ordering Information:

Special discounts are available on quantity purchases by corporations, associations, educators, and others. For details, contact the publisher at the above listed address.

U.S. trade bookstores and wholesalers: Please contact Stacie Baker at staciebaker2017@gmail.com

Dedication

To my sweet husband, Justin:
Thank you for choosing to spend your life with me. I was immensely blessed to be your wife, and although I wish we had our fifty years together, you continue to push me and challenge me in so many ways, even after your death. No matter where life takes me, I will continue loving you for the rest of my days.

Acknowledgements

To my friends and family:

Thank you for consistently supporting me as I navigated life as a young widow. You have supported me, prayed for me, and helped me walk through the most difficult season of my life. It is because of you that this book has come to fruition.

Preface

If you have lost a spouse, this book is for you.

If you have gone through divorce, this book is for you.

If you have lost a child, this book is for you.

If you are grieving in any form, this book is for you.

Maybe you are not currently grieving. Maybe you have never lost someone special to you. I believe you can still find hope in this book. It is my prayer you do.

My name is Stacie Baker, and I became widowed at 25 years old. My husband's name was Justin, and we were married for five months. His death came as a complete shock, which I will go into detail further into this book.

For now, I want you to know that you are not alone on this journey of grief. I, myself, have experienced the tribulations that are attached to losing your best friend. I have cried myself to sleep. I have gone days without eating a real meal. I have yelled and screamed until my voice was hoarse. I have questioned God. I have mourned until I was in physical pain. But, through everything, I have found joy. I have found peace. I have found happiness. I have found myself, and you can too.

Shortly after Justin died, I started researching books written by young widows. I wanted to know that I was not the only twenty-something who lost her husband. I found several helpful books, which I have listed at the end of this book. However, I noticed a trend with each book I picked up. While the books I read were extremely helpful in processing my grief, they were all written several years post-loss. Because of that, I felt like I was missing something, although I could not explain what that was.

So, after about a month into my journey as a widow, I decided to start a blog. I came up with the penname of the Newly Widowed Newlywed. This blog was my platform to document my journey into widowhood as I was experiencing it. Through this, the grief was very present and fresh. I wanted people reading my blogs to find hope in the valleys of life.

So, back to this book. I have compiled the majority of my blog posts together to show how I have progressed through my grief. This book is my story. It is a self-narration of my trials in the first year of widowhood, as well as the successes and accomplishments I came to know.

This story is real. This story is mine. This is the story of how I came back from broken.

Our Story – December 3, 2017

Five months after marrying the man of my dreams, I had so many things I was looking forward to: Our first Christmas as a married couple, starting a family one day, growing old together. One thing I wasn't expecting? Becoming a widow.

Justin and I got married in June of 2017. We dated for three years prior, and I was truly blessed by every minute with him. He was a competitive runner. Justin would always say he used running to glorify God. He was always trying to help others in any way he could, and using his God given talent of running for the Lord was his most common method. On November 14, he went out for a run. Nothing out of the ordinary; he had run thousands of miles in his life. About half a mile from our home, while finishing up his run, he suddenly collapsed. Cardiac arrest. The paramedics exhausted their efforts to get his heart going again. About twenty minutes later, his heart was once again beating, but he was unconscious and unresponsive. We faced many unknowns. We stayed by his side for a week in ICU, until his time on earth came to an end.

Widowed. Just like that, my marriage to the most incredible person I've ever known was over.

To this day there are still unknowns. I would be lying if I said I haven't been angry at God. How could He take Justin away so soon? Our dreams for the future were shattered.

Yes I've been angry. Yes I've been sad. I know I will continue to feel this way for a long time to come. However, something kind of beautiful has come out of this tragedy. During the weeklong stay in the hospital, both of our families were met with an overwhelming amount of love, support, and prayers. Justin's story has literally reached THOUSANDS of people, and his testimony continues to touch lives even after his passing. I have had complete strangers send me messages saying how my strength and faith has inspired them to take a look at their own walk with God. People have been inspired to change their lives for the better because of my husband's unexpected journey.

I can't even put into words how much I miss my husband. I'm not sure I ever will be able to find the words for it. However, I know I have to keep pushing forward. Step by step. Moment by moment. His life on earth may be over, but his life with Christ continues, and his legacy continues. Therefore, I must continue.

What Not to Say to Someone Who is Grieving – December 10, 2017

I want to start off by saying that since Justin was in the hospital, both our families and I have had an INCREDIBLE amount of support from families, friends, and even strangers! I have had many people reach out to help in any way they can, whether it be bringing dinners, sending cards and messages, or even just letting me know they continue to think and pray for us during this time. It's just been amazing.

With that said, there have been a few things on my mind. I have noticed a few words and phrases that may not be the best thing to say to someone who is grieving. This is not to call anyone out by any means, but rather to help people know there are better alternatives on what to say or do.

1. "I know exactly what you are going through."

I know this sounds pretty good to say, but honestly, no you don't. Unless you have lost your husband five months after marrying him, you don't know what I'm going through. And honestly? Half the time, I don't even know.

A better way to get your point across than using this phrase could be to say something like, "I know what it is like to lose someone so close to me." It's possible to have the empathy of losing a loved one without going through the exact same stories. In my opinion, no two stories of grief are the same, so we should stop pretending they are.

2. "If you need anything, you let me know."

Again, this sounds good in theory, but this can easily become an empty promise of one isn't careful. I know I have used this phrase in the past, but now that I'm the one grieving, I have really been thinking hard about this one.

It is hard to know what to say to someone when they're going through one of the hardest times of their life, I get it. But this phrase puts more pressure on the one grieving in the first place. This puts pressure on them to ask for specific ways to help, many of which probably wouldn't ask at all because it may be an inconvenience to someone else.

Instead of putting that pressure on the person you're trying to help in the first place, be more specific. Offer to take them out to lunch, go rake up their leaves, show kindness without asking permission to do so. Even if you're just getting that person out of the house for a few hours, I can almost guarantee they will be very thankful. I have had so many people be there for me in these ways, and it has been a true blessing.

3. "I'm so sorry for your loss."

My 8 year-old sister was actually the one that caught on to this phrase. I myself had never really thought much about it, but she was actually on to something. Again, this can be a phrase that people use when they don't know what else to say. Again: IT IS OK TO NOT KNOW WHAT TO SAY. For me, I don't want people to feel sorry for me and my loss. My loss has been Heaven's gain, and I know Justin is no longer suffering. It is often hard to focus on that, but this is what gives me peace when I think about the fact that Justin is gone.

Instead of saying that you are sorry for my loss, try something like, "I have been praying for you." Or just share your favorite memory about the person who has died. For my family and me, it has been the wonderful stories about Justin that have brought the most smiles in this difficult time. In the last few weeks, we have heard countless stories about Justin that we never even knew about! It has been such a joy to see and hear how many lives he has impacted just by the stories we have been told.

Again, this is NOT to call anyone out. I can speak for both families when I say we have had INCREDIBLE support over the past month, and I am so incredibly thankful. My hope for everyone reading is to maybe think twice about what you say to someone who is grieving.

Gearing up for Christmas without You – December 12, 2017

Justin and I were so excited for Christmas to come. We were both huge fans of this time of year: Christmas lights, spending time with family, Christmas movies and music. We loved it all.

After we got married this summer, we were particularly excited for our first Christmas as a married couple. We looked forward to being in our home together, making it a winter wonderland and enjoying the quality time spent together near the Christmas tree. Little did I know that day would never come.

Justin has been gone for almost a month now, which is crazy to think about. I still catch myself turning to tell him something, checking to see if he has texted me, or thinking about what our plans look like for the night. The only problem is he isn't here anymore.

While I never expected my first Christmas married to Justin to turn into my first Christmas as a widow, I continue to hold on to a few rays of hope.

First, I still have the support of my family and friends. This one has held true since the first night Justin was in the hospital. The people I am surrounded by have been such an incredible support system: I am constantly being checked on by loved ones, and that provides so much comfort in these hard times. These are the people who have helped me through each day.

Second, I hold onto the love Justin and I had for this season. Knowing how much he looked forward to our first Christmas keeps me going. I think he would have done the same if the situation was reversed. Because of his love for Christmas, I have placed myself in a position of celebrating in a way I believe Justin would have celebrated. It makes me feel like he is with me.

Finally, I cling to the knowledge of the real reason for the season. You see, while Watching Christmas movies and opening presents Christmas morning is great, it is not the reason we were meant to celebrate. We celebrate Christmas to remember that Jesus was born to one day bear the weight of our sins. Because of such a sacrifice, we are able to commit our lives to God. Justin did this with the life he was given on earth. Because of his faith in God's promises, I have peace and comfort knowing Justin is spending this Christmas in the most wonderful place imaginable: he is spending Christmas at the feet of our Savior.

I'm not going to sit here and pretend that life without Justin is easy. It's not.

Losing my husband is by far the hardest thing I have dealt with in my life, but knowing where his faith was during his lifetime gives me incredible hope: hope that, because my faith is also in God, I will see him again one day.

This Christmas, I encourage three things for you to do:

1) Spend time with your loved ones. The holidays can be stressful, especially with lots of people around. However, times like this are not promised, so take every opportunity you can to be with the ones you love.

2) Remember the real reason for the season. Read the true story of Christmas from the One who sent His son. Teach your children of the birth of Jesus, as well as the life of Jesus.

3) Hug your loved ones extra tight every chance you get, just in case you run out of chances.

Running Towards the Prize- December 21, 2017

My husband Justin was a remarkable runner. He ran competitively for over ten years of his life. In fact, he even qualified to run in the 2018 Boston Marathon. Running was Justin's form of therapy. It was his time where he could focus and reflect on all sorts of subjects: how life was going, what he planned on doing with friends and family, etc. His biggest part of running was that it was when he could really focus on his walk (or run) with God.

I have never been much of a runner. While I enjoy it (for the most part), I consider myself to be very slow and never commit the time and energy to it like Justin did. One thing I am running towards is a stronger relationship with God. He has been the one to give me the strength to get through each day since Justin's passing. I owe it all to Him, for I know I could not have made it this far without God.

Justin was one of the most selfless people I have ever known. He would ALWAYS put others' needs before his own. Up until his last breath, he lived his life devoted to God.

Since Justin died, I find myself praying more, reading my bible more, and worshipping more. I know where my strength comes from, and I will give glory to the One who keeps me strong. Until my last breath, I will continue to run towards the ultimate prize, just as my late husband did.

I have fought the good fight, I have finished the race, and I have kept the faith - 2 Timothy 4:7-8

The Resolution- December 24, 2017

At the start of this year, Justin and I were talking about New Year's Resolutions. Neither of us had ever made one, but we talked about the whole idea. Eventually, I came up with one: I chose to run a 5k every month for the entire 2017 year. I would try to run a few times a week. I started out strong, getting my runs in like I intended to. After the wedding, the weather got hot, and I was losing the motivation that carried me through the first part of the year. Seeing my lack of motivation, Justin took it upon himself to give me a push: he told me he would run the last race of the year with me. This definitely inspired me to keep pushing. We had been together for nearly four years and never competed in the same race. I wanted to experience that race together, so I told him okay. I so looked forward to participating in a 5k with my husband this December.

We didn't make it to December.

Since Justin's death, I have taken an entirely new outlook on life. What's my conclusion?

Life. Is. Too. Short.

Has there been something you've wanted to do? Something you've wanted to try? Don't put it off. Life's too short.

This time of year, it is so common for many of us to set a resolution for ourselves, whether it be to lose weight, save money, or make amends with people in our lives. Often times, for whatever the reason, these resolutions aren't accomplished.

After Justin's death, I now see that we should not wait for the start of every New Year to try something new, or to set new goals for ourselves. Want to change your lifestyle for the better? Start now. Want to turn over a new leaf with family members? Start now. Thinking of going on a mission trip? Start now.

The way I see it, if we allow ourselves to wait for the New Year every year to set goals for ourselves, we put off valuable time that could've been used to reach said goals all along. The time to change our lives for the better starts now. Don't wait for the New Year.

Start now.

"For I know the plans I have for you" — this is the Lord's declaration — "plans for your welfare, not for disaster, to give you a future and a hope." - Jeremiah 29:11 HCSB

Embracing the New Year- January 6, 2018

2018.

Justin and I had so many plans for 2018. We talked about remodeling our house, embarking on weekend getaways, and starting a family one day. We planned for all of these to begin in 2018.

Now that I am facing this New Year without Justin by my side, my plans look completely different. Since we lost Justin back in November, I have learned several lessons along the way.

1. Although my husband is gone, I am not alone.

I know I have said it before, but I have been completely overwhelmed by how many people have checked on me since Justin's accident. The amount of love, prayers and support from everyone has shown me that while my husband is gone, I am not alone. I have the love and encouragement coming from so many friends and family, and most importantly, I have God. He has been the One that has given me peace during the hardest days of my life.

2. My plans now look different.

Yes, Justin and I had plans for the New Year. As I said before, we had talked about what the New Year would bring us. Now that he is gone, I have learned that life is short. I've learned that I want to travel and see more of the world. I've learned that I'm stronger than I originally thought. I've learned that I'm capable of so much more than I give myself credit for. For 2018, I now plan to give more, travel more, and rely on God more. I plan to best the best I can be.

3. I can choose to embrace the New Year.

I am left with two options. I can either use my grief as an excuse to seclude myself and not talk to anyone, OR I can use my grief as a reason to try new things.

Of these two options, I choose the latter. I consider myself an introvert, so it is very easy for me to choose to stay home all the time. Instead, I'm choosing to embrace this New Year. I want to spend more time with friends and family. I want to travel to new places. I want to go on another mission trip someday. Golly, I may even choose to take ice skating lessons, just to try something new.

I think about the plans Justin and I had for this New Year quite often still. Plans change, even when we don't expect them to. My story is living proof of that. Although it is hard to admit sometimes, I know that God always has a plan, and His plans never fail. I cling to this in times of unknowns. I will continue to keep pushing forward.

Growing up, I feel like my idea of a widow was pretty similar to many ideas out there: old, weak, secluded, grouchy.

I'll be the first to admit that I thought of the above definition for the longest time. I can remember seeing movies and reading stories as a child; this was often how widows were portrayed.

Since losing Justin, I have been focusing a lot of my time and energy soaking up inspiration from other widows: Blogs, social media posts, or just messaging ones I know personally. I have learned that widows are some of the strongest people I know.

The reason? They are living without the one person they thought they could never live without. I'll not hesitate to admit I still have moments where I break down in the comfort of my own home. This doesn't make us weak– it makes us more aware than ever of what matters so deeply to us.

Yes, it is incredibly difficult. I no longer wake up next to my husband and I am reminded daily (in many ways) that he is no longer with me, and I have no choice in that. I have to keep moving forward. Step by step. Widows/widowers are strong. We come in all ages and walks of life. We have good days, as well as bad.

Shortly after Justin passed, I was filling out some paperwork. I remember getting to the part where I have to check the box defining my marital status. For the first time, I had to check the box marked "Widowed." It was extremely difficult. For the most part, I have come to terms with what has happened, and have accepted the unfortunate fact that I've lost my best friend.

I will always miss Justin. That's never going to change, and I know that. However, I can choose to be secluded and shut everyone around me out, just as I used to think of widows, or I can help redefine the term. I can choose to be strong. I can choose to move forward. I can choose.

Learning to Use Grief as a Reason, and not as an Excuse – January 21, 2018

Since losing my husband two months ago today, I have been on a roller coaster of emotions. I have good days, I have bad days, and I have days where I don't even know what I'm feeling. I have also had days where I want to sit in my dark and empty house and not talk to anyone. There have been days where I have used my grief process as an excuse to not do things. I have most frequently used it as an excuse not to take care of myself at times.

It would be so easy for me to use my grief as an excuse to not work out, or to not eat healthy. And to be honest? At times I've done both. However, I have learned that taking better care of myself has helped my grieving process. So, I'm using my grief as a reason- not as an excuse.

I use my grief as a reason to exercise more.

My husband was so athletic. I always envied his ability to run fast and far! While I know I will never be the runner he was, I can still run. I can still swim. I can still lift weights. I can still be stronger, and I intend to be. There are some days where I just need to relax, and I recognize that, but I also know how great it feels to conquer a workout, so I push myself more to reach that feeling of conquering the day.

I use my grief as a reason to eat healthier.

Justin died of cardiac arrest. While we didn't ever find out what caused his cardiac arrest, I have learned that it is so important to take care of yourself. Justin was one of the healthiest people I knew, and if he can just suddenly go into cardiac arrest while running, what is stopping the rest of us from battling with other health problems? This is something I can help prevent by eating healthier. While those sugary sweets taste yummy and make you feel good at first, there is often an undeniable presence of regret to follow. I am learning ways to eat healthier to promote a happier me. Losing a loved one is not an excuse to lose control of our own health. If anything, it is a reason to take better care of ourselves so we can be there for our other loved ones during the hardest times.

I will use my grief as a reason to travel more.

Since becoming widowed, I have learned that life is too short to simply wish to see the world. Instead of sitting at home wishing to see new sights, I am using my grief as a reason to travel more and see new places, rather than dreaming about them.

God has created a beautiful world, and I plan to use more of my time to see more of it. I feel closest to God when I am in the midst of his wondrous creations, so I plan on spending a lot more time with Him in the middle of it all.

I know I will continue to have both good and bad days, but by using my grief as a reason to push myself, I know I can make it through the toughest days to come.

May the Lord of peace Himself give you peace always in every way. The Lord be with all of you. - 2 Thessalonians 3:16

Dealing with the Tough Days- January 23, 2018

I'm writing this with tears in my eyes. Why? Because it's been a tough day.

Though the tough days don't come as often anymore, they still come, and can come full-force. On the days I miss Justin most, I feel so many emotions: sometimes more than I realize.

If only we knew when the tough days were coming. Unfortunately, there is no schedule for these kinds of things. The tough days often come without warning. If you have dealt with losing something or someone important to you, you may know the feeling.

For me, my tough days typically start off good. In fact, I may not break down until the end of the day. But when it hits, it hits me hard. I can ugly cry until my face hurts. I can yell and scream in the privacy of my home. I can get angry at God (and I have!)

That last one can be hard to admit. "Angry at God? I'm not allowed to be angry at God."
Sound familiar?

It's easy to catch ourselves being angry at God, and it's easy to feel guilty for that. But here's the thing:

God can handle our anger.

God can handle our fears.

God can handle our toughest days, and God can handle our tears.

I have had so many people tell me how strong and inspirational I have been through all of this, and please hear me when I say I appreciate those kind words so much! However, I feel it is just as important to show that I don't always have it together. I do break down. I do have tough days.

If you are going through some of your toughest days, or you're angry at God, please know that God can handle it. If you need to cry until your face hurts (like I do on occasion), do it. Sometimes we just have to allow ourselves to have those tough days. It's all part of a process. When we are able to turn to Him for strength, we begin to see better days ahead.

"He heals the brokenhearted and binds up their wounds."- Psalms 147:3 HCSB

Five Things to Discuss with your Loved Ones Right Now- January 28, 2018

No one ever wants to talk about death. Honestly? It's not fun to talk about. When considering your best friend, your spouse, or a beloved family member, the mere thought of losing them can sometimes be too much to bear. I know for me, the thought of losing my husband, even years down the road, was difficult. I couldn't imagine my life without him.

Unfortunately, I lost him five months into our marriage.

We had just started our lives together. We talked about the positive things we expected would come in the future: kids, job promotions, family trips. While all this provided great discussion points, we avoided questions that weren't as fun: we never talked about what would happen if one of us died.

And I am sure this isn't surprising. What newlyweds want to talk about losing their spouse right after getting married? I get it. It's hard to talk about, but you may never get the chance to talk about it.

Whether your single, married, or in a relationship, I encourage you to talk about the following topics with those you are closest with, and I recommend doing it now.

1. Get Life Insurance

Justin and I talked about getting life insurance, but we never chose a plan. Now of course, I so wish we had just sat down one afternoon and done it. It is not a long and grueling process. Ask other families what policies they use. Whatever you do, do not stop talking about it until you decide together on a life insurance policy. There are so many affordable policies out there that will fit your family's needs if something unexpected were to happen.

2. Discuss funeral plans.

This is probably one of the most morbid topics on my list. However, your loved ones will have no way of knowing what type of funeral/burial you prefer unless you TALK ABOUT IT. Furthermore, planning a funeral for a loved one is difficult when you are in the middle of grieving. It's hard to think straight most of the time, and planning a funeral can add so much more stress. It was so hard to plan my husband's funeral. Luckily, I wasn't alone. Both his family and my family stayed by my side through it all. Still, we had no way of really knowing what Justin would've done differently.

If the day comes and something happens to you, your significant other will have a better idea on how you want to be memorialized. Talk about where you would want to be buried, what kind of service you would want, etc. Also, be sure to write it all down!

3. Create a will.

Again, this is not something Justin and I ever came close to discussing. If there are certain items you want certain friends or family members to have, write it in your will. If you own a lot of possessions, it is very important to document your wishes. This will help reduce the stress on the family of figuring out what to do with your belongings after you pass.

4. Discuss what would happen if one of you dies unexpectedly.

Have a plan in place for the unimaginable. Have a family meeting where you discuss where all of the important documents are. Talk about when bills are due, and how they are paid each month. Write down any usernames or passwords for online accounts. Keep all of this together somewhere safe. If something did happen to you, you wouldn't want your loved ones to go on multiple scavenger hunts just to find some necessary documents.

But also talk about your lives together. Would you want your spouse to remarry if you died unexpectedly? Most people would probably say yes to that, but take the time to really talk about it.

5. Tell that person how much you love them.

The bottom line is we are not promised tomorrow. Take time to really express to your loved ones just how much you love them. I'm so thankful that Justin and I discussed this constantly. Not a day in our marriage went by without us saying how much we loved each other. Losing Justin has been so difficult. Some days are better than others, but after losing him, I am confident he knew how I felt about him. I told him every day, on multiple occasions, how much I loved him, and he did the same. Had we not taken the time to share that with each other, I would be regretting all of the missed opportunities.

As I said before, we are not promised tomorrow.

Trust me.

I know these are not exactly exciting topics to discuss, but it is so important to prepare for the unimaginable.

"Many plans are in a man's heart, but the Lord's decree will prevail." - Proverbs 19:21 HCSB

A Letter to my Deceased Husband – February 4, 2018

My love,

There are so many things I wish I would have said to you had I known your last breath was near. I missed my chance on a lifetime of happiness with you. Things will absolutely never be the same without you by my side, but I take comfort in knowing you're resting and rejoicing in heaven. Still, so much remains on my mind since losing you.

My hope is that you know just how much I loved you. I constantly think back to our wedding just over seven months ago, and think about how incredibly wonderful everything was. It wasn't the perfect day because of the dress I wore or the cake we had. It was the perfect day because I was able to stand in front of friends and family with you: we read our vows and made promises we hoped to keep for a long time. While your life was cut short, I still look at your handwritten vows often, and think to myself how incredibly lucky I was to have even gotten five months of marriage with you. I hope you knew just how much I loved you.

I wish we had talked about our future more. When one gets married, it is easy to think in-the-moment. I wish we had the chance to talk more about our lives down the road.

I wish I could have had just one more hug and kiss from you. At the end of each day, I would come home and the day would never feel complete until I was in your arms once again. Had I known the last time I was going to be in your arms, I would have never let go.

I wish I could tell you how proud I was of all you've accomplished. You were the hardest working man I knew, and you always put others before yourself. That was one of the many reasons I fell in love with you in the first place.

I wish I could tell you that even though you're no longer with me, I still think of you. You never leave my mind. Since the night of your accident, I've dreamt about you almost every night. You're gone, but even still you're always with me.

Loved you yesterday, love you still. Always have, always will.

Love,

Your Sunshine

A Letter to the Future Me – February 11, 2018

Dear Future Me,

As life continues without Justin, there are some things I want you to remember, whether it's six months down the road, a year down the road, or ten years down the road:

1. Keep Living for God

You have been able to share your story with thousands of people since Justin's accident in November 2017. People have seen your walk with God as you've embarked on this difficult journey, and they draw strength from you. Don't ever forget that. Continue first and foremost to use your story to spread the Word of God. Don't ever lose sight of this.

2. Keep Trying New Things

Do not be afraid to step out of your comfort zone from time to time. Life is too short to sit on the sidelines! Get out in nature, see new sites, try new things. I know you've been trying to travel more, so go somewhere you've never been before.

3. Don't Let Guilt Set In

Down the road, you may find that you're actually finding joy in life again. You may not grieve like you used to, or as much as you used to. That is ok. In fact, it is bound to happen in time. Do NOT feel guilty for living life after loss. It's ok to be happy! We are not created to live in a constant state of guilt. Life goes on, even after loss (as hard as it is to admit sometimes).

4. Do Not Be Afraid of the Future

Obviously, we do not know what the future holds, but one thing is certain: this journey you've have been on has made you so much stronger than you thought you were capable of being. You have grown so much closer to God, as well as friends and family. You have built new friendships after Justin's death. Whatever the future may hold for you, do not be afraid. God has a plan for you yet.

"Lord, you are my portion and my cup of blessing; you hold my future."- Psalm 16:5 HCSB

A Story on Grief- February 14, 2018

Grief does not discriminate.

It doesn't care where you grew up, what your favorite animal is, or where you went to school.

Grief does not care about your background, beliefs, or future plans.

Grief can come and visit at any time, even when it's not invited. Grief doesn't care. It comes anyways, nearly breaking down the door to your life.

Grief doesn't care if you have been married fifty years, five months, or not at all. Grief doesn't care if you have kids or grandkids, or what kind of car you drive.

Grief is exhausting, and often excruciating. When the world smiles, Grief says not to. When the world laughs, Grief says to stop.

But....

Grief does not have permission to overtake me. Grief is part of a process we all eventually come to know. However, grief will not win.

I have overcome hardships and difficulties in life. This is by far the hardest. I am supposed to be living life as a newlywed right now, but I'm facing life widowed.

Grief will not win. It can come and visit from time to time, but it cannot obtain a permanent residence in my life. I know God has plans for me still, and whatever they may be, grief will not stop me.

"I am weary from grief; strengthen me through Your word." - Psalms 119:28 HCSB

Small Victories- February 18, 2018

When I lost Justin back in November, I was experiencing a multitude of emotions. I rejoiced that he was resting in heaven with the Lord, yet at the same time I was angry because I felt like I was robbed of a wonderful future. I was sad because my best friend was gone. A lot of the time I even felt numb- just due to the fact that I didn't know how I was feeling at times.

While it is hard to get through some days without Justin by my side, I have recently chosen to reflect on the small victories that have occurred since his passing. This was NOT easy to do. In fact, when I first sat down to write this list, I had nothing. Then, all of a sudden, I began to write. These are my small victories so far:

1. I have drawn closer to God.

This is a big victory to me, but I felt I needed to start the list off with this. Since everything that happened with Justin nearly three months ago, I have done more praying than I have ever done. I prayed for Justin to get better, yes, but I have also prayed for strength, I've prayed for my family, Justin's family (though they are still my family too), and really just anyone that knew him. I've prayed that his story would continue to inspire others to live life to the fullest.

Through everything, my relationship with the Lord is stronger than it has ever been. That's victory in Jesus.

2. I painted my kitchen.

Justin and I had plans to remodel our kitchen this year. Though he is not around to see it, I decided to put our plans into action. The first step was to paint the kitchen. I was amazed at how much better I felt just by slapping on a fresh coat of paint. It was like a breath of fresh air! Although the kitchen remodel is far from completed, this was the first step- a small victory.

3. I sat in our chair.

In our living room, there is a couch and an oversized chair with an ottoman. Justin and I ALWAYS sat together on this chair. In the five months we were married, we probably used the couch just a handful of times.

After Justin died, I couldn't bring myself to sit in the chair. I always would choose the couch. I think in a way, I avoided the chair because I wanted to avoid one more validation that Justin isn't here anymore. For this chair, it meant I would be sitting in it alone. However, for the first time in almost three months, I've sat in our chair. Victory.

4. I have learned how to change the air filters in my house.

This one seems silly, but it was something Justin would take care of. When the time came to replace them, I had no clue what I was doing. I was lucky I found the filters in the first place! But I changed them. Victory.

Sometimes, we life gets hard, we need to keep track of the small victories we accomplish in our lives. I could add more to this list, but these stuck out to me the most.

Maybe you are dealing with the loss of a loved one. Perhaps you can't find a job to support your family. Or, maybe life is just too hard right now, even if you can't quite put your finger on why. Please remember: it is small victories like these that get us through the hardest of times. Though the victories may seem small, they add up overtime, and sooner or later it becomes easier to spot. So, whatever you may be dealing with, I encourage you to stop what you're doing right now, grab a pen and some paper, and right down your small victories. I would love to hear what you come up with!

"But thanks be to God, who gives us the victory through our Lord Jesus Christ! Therefore, my dear brothers, be steadfast, immovable, always excelling in the Lord's work, knowing that your labor in the Lord is not in vain."- 1 Corinthians 15:57-58

Healing Steps- February 25, 2018

Over the past few months I have learned this: grief is so hard to understand, even when you're submerged in the depths of it. There is no timeline for grieving, despite what some may say. You may take two steps forward one day only to take three steps back later. It's inexplicable.

One thing I have learned through my grieving process is I always feel better after a workout. Exercise has been such a helpful tool to release tension built up from grief. Until today, I have yet to go for a run since Justin died.

As I mentioned last week, I have been hesitant to go for a run. Justin went into cardiac arrest while running, so I have been scared to get back out there myself. While I was nowhere near the runner Justin was, it was still something I enjoyed.

After Justin died, I was terrified to exercise at all. Eventually, I was able to go for a swim or hop on the rowing machine. But running? Running still terrified me. Running was what put my loving husband of five months into cardiac arrest. What if something bad happened to me while I was running too? I was living in fear.

Now, I have a choice to make. I can be cautious with every little task I do, living my life in fear, OR I can still get out and do things I enjoyed doing before.

For the first time in over three months, I went on my first run this morning. It wasn't easy, but each step is helping me grow. Each step is helping me process things. Each step helps me connect with my late husband, who loved running so much. Each step is offering me healing steps toward a future. A bright future. And I thank God for the courage I have moving forward each day.

"But those who trust in the Lord will renew their strength; they will soar on wings like eagles; they will run and not grow weary; they will walk and not faint." - Isaiah 40:31 HCSB

Self Check: In this moment RIGHT NOW, how are you? What are you struggling with? What are you overcoming? Use the lines below to jot down some personal insight.

_____

_____

_____

_____

_____

_____

_____

_____

_____

_____

_____

Extinguishing the Guilt- March 4, 2018

Does anyone else feel guilty for the most ridiculous things? I know I have!

For me, I have felt a lot of guilt lately. I have felt guilty for smiling, laughing, and finding joy in the little things again. For me, there are times when I think to myself, "My husband is dead. What do I have to be happy about?"

In reality, we weren't created to live in a constant state of guilt and grief.

Justin has been gone for going on four months now. Life is slowly returning to a state of "normal," even though it will never be the same without him. And while I miss Justin deeply, and still think of him every day, I know that I must continue on. I cannot let myself feel guilty for that.

So, while it is sometimes hard, I know that when that guilt sneaks into my life I must extinguish it. If the tables were turned, and it was Justin here living without me, I wouldn't want him to feel guilty for a moment for living life to its fullest without me. I think he would want the same for me.

When guilt sneaks into your life, you must ask yourself: 1) am I going to welcome this guilt in and allow it to consume me, or 2) am I going to choose to extinguish this guilt and live life the best ways I know how?

It may not happen suddenly, but I hope you learn to extinguish the guilt in your life. It is then when you can continue to live life to its fullest.

"Dear friend, I pray that you may prosper in every way and be in good health physically just as you are spiritually." - 3 John 1:2 HCSB

Courageous vs. Cautious- March 11, 2018

I remember the weeks following Justin's death, I was so cautious with everything I did: I avoided running, working out, or any scenario where I could get hurt. I was living my life cautiously. And honestly, it was hard to function for a while.

When we live life in a state of extreme caution, we can miss out on some really great opportunities. Because I was living this way, I was missing out on chances to better myself.

When I started running last week, I realized how silly it is to live cautiously! *Note: there are some times where caution helps us, so be smart*

Yes, bad things happen in life (I will attest to that), but we can't live life avoiding good opportunities in our lives just because we fear the bad things that could happen.

Slowly but surely, I have started challenging myself in different ways. I have started working out again, little by little. Before Justin's death, I loved trying all sorts of activities. Overtime, I have been able to get back to that. I'm not the same person I was before Justin's death, and that's ok. It will be ok. I will be ok. In time.

It sounds silly, but the other day I was watching The Princess Diaries, and at one point a character says this:

"The brave may not live forever, but the cautious do not live at all."

Wow. Did I ever need to hear that!

With the life I have left, whether long or short, I'm not going to live in fear. I'm going to take chances, go on adventures, live life to the fullest, and do what I enjoy.

I hope you do the same.

"Therefore, take courage, men, because I believe God that it will be just the way it was told to me."- Acts 27:25 HCSB

Moving Forward- March 18, 2018

"In time, Stacie, you will move on from this."

Boy, am I sick of hearing that.

People try to say the right thing to someone grieving, and they come from good intentions, but this one just bothers me.

Why? Because I don't want to move on. Moving on, to me, implies I will one day just get over what I've endured. I don't want to just get over losing Justin. The pain of losing a loved one doesn't just go away. When I am told that I'll "get over" losing him, it feels like he wouldn't be important enough to remember.

This is so far from the truth. To me, I don't want to move on. Instead I am choosing to move forward. I loved Justin so much. I still do. I always will.

Moving forward is different from moving on: by moving forward, I am continuing to live life, but I 100% recognize the empty chair at the dinner table. I notice the empty house when I come home from work. The empty feeling I have from losing Justin is real. I recognize that, and I feel emotions from that. However, I do know that life goes on.

Because of the love we had, I choose to move forward: still continuing to think about him, still continuing to love him, but still continuing to put my life back together, piece by piece. The only difference is that the puzzle is looking different now. The pieces of the puzzle fit differently now. But I will never move on from loving and losing Justin.

I'm moving forward.

"A man who endures trials is blessed, because when he passes the test he will receive the crown of life that God has promised to those who love Him." - James 1:12 HCSB

When it seems your Prayers go Unanswered- March 25, 2018

For the entire week Justin was hospitalized before his death, we had hundreds of people lifting up hundreds of prayers for Justin to get better. We prayed nonstop.

He never left the hospital.

In this particular season, it was so hard to figure out why God never answered these prayers. Justin was an incredible person, so why wouldn't God heal him?

It's easy for us to praise God when things go right in life, but what about when things go not as planned? That's when we forget to praise God. And it's not hard to see why. I don't know about you, but when things seem to go wrong, praise is not the first thing I do.

At church last week, we were in the book of Job. Job praised and thanked God for all of the blessings in his life. Satan said the only reason he could praise God was because he hadn't experienced tragedies in life. So, he tested Job. He took everything that mattered away from Job.

Instead of blaming God, he continued to praise God. Wow. Job could have chosen to turn away from God, but he knew it was in those moments he would need God the most. Don't get me wrong; Job cried out to God, but he never blamed God.

While Justin never made it from the hospital, I can still praise God for several things:

1) I praise God that Justin knew the Lord. Because of this relationship, I know he is logging his running miles in heaven!

2) I praise God that I got to know Justin. While we were only married for five months, we knew each other for about five years. To be able to look back from when we first met to how our love story played out over time is such a gift to me I will continue to cherish.

3) Justin's death has allowed others to develop or renew their relationship with the Lord. I have had several people message me over the last few months saying how their lives have changed from hearing of Justin's story. To me, that's amazing!

The bottom line: just because we don't think God has answered our prayers, doesn't mean he hasn't. It just means that perhaps He has answered them in a different way. Or, perhaps he just hasn't answered them yet. That is where patience comes in handy, but that is for another week.

Now, back to Job. When Job continued to praise God, despite the tragedies in his own life, God blessed him with twice as much as he had before.

Whenever it feels like God is ignoring your prayers, take a minute to think about what you're really praying for. Then take a minute to remember: just because God doesn't answer our prayers in the format we hoped for, doesn't mean He doesn't answer them at all. He answers every prayer, and He is not finished with you yet. God may still be working on you.

And He is working on me still.

"The Lord gives, and the Lord takes away. Praise the name of Yahweh. Throughout all this Job did not sin or blame God for anything." - Job 1:21-22 HCSB

I'm Glad You Chose Me Still- March 26, 2018

Only married for five months,
Our future seemed so bright.
Then, all of a sudden you were gone.
No one to kiss good night.
We talked about our future plans.
Now we never will.
But even though you are gone
I'm glad you chose me still.

Never again will I hold your hand.
No more will you kiss my cheek.
I press forward, when I can
With each passing week.
Sometimes the pain of losing you makes me physically ill;
But even in the midst of that, I'm glad you chose me still.

I know you're rejoicing in Heaven until we reunite.
But until then it's just me.
In time I'll be alright.
This time apart is temporary, for I know Heaven is for real.
For even when we reunite
I'll be glad you chose me still.

Risen- April 1, 2018

As time continues to pass, more and more holidays have come and gone since Justin passed away. Seasons have passed. I have experienced my first Thanksgiving, Christmas, and Valentine's Day without my husband by my side.

Today, Easter joined the list.

However, sadness is not accompanying this day. Today, we rejoice.

We rejoice for the meaning of Easter. God sent His own son to die in place of our sin, just so he could rise three days later. Those who believe this will live eternally, according to His word.

Jesus. Has. Risen.

Because Jesus died and rose from the grave, and because Justin lived his life following the Lord, he gets to spend Easter Sunday with JESUS.

My goodness.

I don't have a long post this week. I guess I'll end with this:

This Easter Sunday, remember that He has risen. Spend today with your closest friends and family.

He. Has. Risen.

"But now Christ has been raised from the dead, the first fruits of those who have fallen asleep. For since death came through a man, the resurrection of the dead also comes through a man. For as in Adam all die, so also in Christ all will be made alive." - 1 Corinthians 15:20-22 HCSB

Waiting for the Next Chapter- April 8, 2018

I don't know about you, but I have always dreamt about my future for as long as I can remember. When I was in high school, I dreamt about what kind of college I would go to. In college, I dreamt about what job I would have and who I would marry.

When I married Justin, we dreamed together. We dreamed about where life would take us, how many kids we would have, and the list goes on.

Since becoming widowed, my future looks different. Since losing Justin, I often wonder what the next chapter of my life will look like. What my future will look like. When it comes down to it, I have no clue. None of us do. So I have been working really hard on appreciating the chapter I am in. This is not exactly easy when my husband died years before my plan expected. But still, I am thankful.

I'm thankful for the time we had together. I'm thankful for the roof over my head. I'm thankful for my wonderful job. I'm thankful for friends and family that care for me and check on me.

The list.

Goes.

On.

Rather than waiting for the next chapter in your life, take a minute to soak up the chapter you're in. Thank God for what you have right now, instead of what you hope to have in the future. When the timing is right, that page will turn. But until then, be thankful for your current chapter in life. Here's the deal: no one is promised tomorrow, so let's start appreciating today.

"Come now, you who say, "Today or tomorrow we will travel to such and such a city and spend a year there and do business and make a profit." You don't even know what tomorrow will bring — what your life will be! For you are like smoke that appears for a little while, then vanishes. Instead, you should say, "If the Lord wills, we will live and do this or that."" - James 4:13-15 HCSB

Seasons- April 15, 2018

Over the weekend, I had the fortunate opportunity to help out with a women's ministry conference at my alma mater. The theme for the weekend was "Seasons," which represented how, in each of our lives, we have our seasons.

I was totally blown away. Prior to this weekend, I thought I knew what season I was currently going through: winter. Winter in our lives can represent death, destruction, and disappointment.

Five months ago, I was pretty sure I had received a one-way ticket to this particular season. Justin had just suffered from cardiac arrest and was on life support. A week later, almost to the hour, I became a widow at 25. Looking back, I had NO CLUE how I was going to live without the man of my dreams. I hated this season.

But I'm still here. By the grace of God.

After the conference, I decided I am past the season where death and destruction in my life has occurred. Instead, I'm experiencing a Spring-like season: growth, change, and a little bit of pain along the way.

In our lives, seasons will come and go, and come again. In those hard seasons, continue to press into God for the strength and wisdom needed to take those healing steps forward.

I'm growing. Changing. Adapting.

Healing.

While I wait for the next season in my life, I will choose to rejoice in God's wonderful promises.

Milestones- April 22, 2018

Milestones.

We typically look at milestones as accomplishments in our lives: crossing the finish line of your first 5K, graduating high school, buying a first home, seeing your children take their first steps, etc. We work hard in life to do well, and hitting those milestones produces a great sense of achievement within.

Milestones look different when you're grieving. These milestones become the first birthday, Holiday, or big family event without that loved one. The milestone may be a personal record of how long you've gone without crying until you're physically hurting. Rather than a sense of complete achievement, they become these constant reminders that our loved one simply is not coming back. These milestones are not fun at all. A milestone I had expected in my life was our first Christmas as a married couple. Instead, it became my first Christmas as a widow. This did not feel like a sense of accomplishment at all, and it was a milestone I did not want in my life.

With all of the pain that accompanies the loss of a loved one, there is still hope- hope that, one day, the pain will lessen. I think back to when we first lost Justin. The pain of losing him was so excruciating, I'm not sure I know a word strong enough to describe it. I had no clue how I was supposed to keep going.

Fast forward to now: Justin has been gone for five months. The pain still presents itself on occasion, but it has weakened. I couldn't think straight before, but I'm able to again (for the most part!). I'm learning how to do things around the house that Justin would have done before. The list goes on.

I think about times where I've ran a 5k. Sometimes I'm feeling good all the way to the end, but there have been other times, harder times, where all I could do was keep moving forward to the next mile. Once I get this far, I tell myself, "ok. Just two more miles to go. Ok, now there's only one more mile." I do this until I cross that finish line and feel that sense of accomplishment. A point of the race where I can say, "I did it!"

The same goes for my milestones now. While they may not have been the milestones I expected in my life, I'm still telling myself to keep going, and when I hit the milestones I've been moving toward, I take a minute to feel that sense of accomplishment.

And I am going to celebrate the heck out of those accomplishments.

My "Whys" – April 29, 2018

When Justin died, I started searching resources for young widows. I was able to find a few great books and websites, but I honestly did not find very much on the matter. I knew I couldn't be the only one widowed at 25, so I decided to do something about it.

I started this blog for several reasons:

1. I wanted to tell my story.

Using this as a platform to share the love Justin and I had for each other has been a great therapeutic tool for me to cope with the loss of my best friend. I can freely write what I'm feeling each week, and share it with the world. Knowing I wasn't the only young widow, I wanted to share my story to reach out and touch the lives of those who may be going through similar circumstances.

2. I wanted to share what grief is really like.

Before I lost Justin, I thought I had a good grip on what grief was like. After losing him, I realized my concept of grief, like many others, was extremely wrong. Grief is raw, physically painful, and absolutely devastating. I wanted people to know what grief was really like, because we all go through grief at some point in our lives.

3. I wanted to inspire.

I have a deep love for helping others. When Justin died, I knew I wanted to help others who are grieving. I wanted to inspire those to keep pushing forward, even in the darkest days of their lives. I wanted people to know that they are not alone, and life can be beautiful even after loss.

4. I wanted to give God the glory.

When a loved one dies, your faith can be easily shaken. For me, knowing that Justin was a Christian, I had peace in mind knowing that I would be reunited with him one day. That is all because of God's sacrifice years ago. He sent His only son to die so we could live eternally if we believe in Him. Even though the future I had originally planned with Justin is never going to happen, I have faith in and trust that the Lord will have a bigger plan for me. My faith in God has strengthened so much on this journey, and for that I thank God.

At this point, I have officially been widowed longer than I was married to Justin. The pain is still there. The grief is still very real. At the same time, I am healing. I am growing. I am moving forward with each passing day. I thank God I was able to be the one Justin spent the last of his life with. If you were ever wondering why I've chosen to publish my thoughts since becoming widowed, these are my "whys."

Be Still- May 6, 2018

I don't know about anyone else, but I have recently felt like my days are going by too fast! Too much to do and not enough time to do it. Anyone else? Hello? Maybe it is just me.

If you're right there with me, then you probably know how the feeling of defeat can trickle in. We work so hard to check things off our list of to-do items, only to focus on what didn't get done. I've really struggled with this lately. Why work so hard to cross things off our list when we focus on what's not crossed off?

The way I see it, we are not giving ourselves enough credit. Furthermore, we aren't giving ourselves enough grace.

I've noticed that I've been so focused on getting everything done, I have neglected my quiet time with God. I wish I could spit out excuses like, "oh it's the end of the school year and I just don't have time," but that's not helping anyone.

Quiet time.

My quiet time typically involves reading a passage or two, listening to some relaxing music, or just praying to God (often outdoors somewhere when it's nice out). It calms me down, helps me refocus the lens on my life, and helps me put things in my life into perspective. When Justin died, I had a LOT of quiet time. I just recently noticed that my quiet time game has not been strong lately, so I am going to make a change.

This week, I am going to really work on giving myself just a little bit of grace when I only cross 8 things off my list instead of 12. I'm going to rejoice when I hit a goal I have been working hard toward for weeks. Above all else, I am going to work on being still and letting God speak to me in my life.

Will you do the same?

"But He said to me, "My grace is sufficient for you, for power is perfected in weakness." Therefore, I will most gladly boast all the more about my weaknesses, so that Christ's power may reside in me." - 2 Corinthians 12:9 HCSB

How to Grieve (The Right Way) – May 20, 2018

If you have lost someone close to you, then you've probably heard people giving their advice on how to grieve. Things like going to counseling, seeking out support groups, and remembering the happy times are typical topics when it comes to figuring out how to grieve. When I lost Justin, I had a hard time learning how to grieve. What was right? What was wrong? I was already lost enough losing my husband of five months, but for some reason I just had a hard time with figuring out with grief looks like for me. Here's what I learned:

There is no one right way to grieve.

I'm going to say that one more time:

There is no one right way to grieve.

What works for me may not work for others and what works for others may not work for me. And that's OK.

For me, something that has helped with my grieving has been turning to God, joining a Griefshare group, and writing this blog. For someone else, it may be helpful for them to play music or to memorialize their loved one in some form or fashion, and that's okay, too. When it comes to how you should grieve, do what's right for you. I can't stress this enough.

Don't let anyone tell you how your grief should look. As long as you're taking good care of yourself in the process, do what you need to do in order to process everything. There is no one right way to grieve.

Please remember that.

"Therefore we do not give up. Even though our outer person is being destroyed, our inner person is being renewed day by day." - 2 Corinthians 4:16

Reflection – May 27, 2018

I have always been one to reflect on my past experiences. I often look back on memories of my childhood, memories of high school and college, and memories of being married to the best man I could have asked for.

I also look back on the worst memories: losing my loving husband of five months. I have flashbacks of that dreaded night we discovered he had suffered from cardiac arrest while running. I think back to the two hours driving in the dark, praying we wouldn't find him in a ditch somewhere (When Justin collapsed, he had no ID on him so he was at the hospital as a John Doe). I think back to the week in the hospital: the ups and downs and turmoil and grief. Many parts of that week are a blur, but I remember the agonizing pain both our families suffered through while waiting for what we prayed wouldn't happen.

These times where I reflect on the pain of losing my husband feels like it is brand new, and at times I feel like I'm reliving the loss of my love. Then I think of Jesus.

The agonizing pain Jesus endured on the cross is unimaginable, but I'm sure God felt the pain of grief, for He gave up His only son to die for our sins. Because of this act, I can choose to live a life for Christ.

Today would have been Justin's 28th birthday, so naturally I'm doing more reflecting. More specifically, I've been reflecting on his birthday last year. We surprised him by inviting many of our friends and family to surprise him in the backyard for a cookout. But, as luck would have it, we eventually lost power due to a thunderstorm.

I remember sitting in the dark surrounded by people that meant so much to both me and Justin. Despite his birthday surprise being a wash-out, it was the perfect evening spent with friends and family.

Today would've been Justin's 28th birthday, but for the first time, he is spending his birthday in Heaven. Some members of both mine and Justin's families are spending the week in Destin to honor his memory. So, on this day, and for the rest of this week, we are choosing to reflect on the life Justin lived. We are choosing to reflect on the man Justin was. We are choosing to have one of his favorite birthday meals in his memory tonight: baked beans and hamburgers.

Something Wonderful – June 10, 2018

Anyone else ever feel like they're waiting for something wonderful to happen?

I catch myself doing this from time to time. I was driving across town the other day, and I pulled up behind a car with a bumper sticker that read, "Something wonderful is to come." This could not have come at a better time. Today, possibly even as you're reading this, I am making the journey to Houston, Texas for a weeklong mission trip. As you probably know, this area was hit hard by Hurricane Harvey last year. And if you really know me, you know I have a heart for Crisis Response trips like this.

As I read this bumper sticker, I immediately thought of this week to come: something wonderful is about to happen. God is moving in this city, and I look forward to being there. I may not know what is in store for the week, but I'm excited. I'm excited because this is the first mission trip I've been on since Justin died (honestly, it's the first one I have been on since we even started dating). I'm excited because I'm going somewhere I've never been before. I'm excited to share the gospel and my testimony with complete strangers. I'm excited because I love helping people in need.

Something wonderful is about to happen. I definitely don't know what it is, but I can't wait to find out. If you have a moment this week, I have a few prayer requests:

1) Please pray for the people of Houston. Pray that they don't lose hope. Pray that they seek the Lord in times of crises.

2) Please pray for the safety of the teams coming down for the week. Pray for their strength and that they won't lose sight of the purpose of the trip.

3) Please pray for me. This is the longest journey I have ever made by myself. Pray that I don't miss my flights and everything runs

smoothly for the trip down and back. Also, pray that God can speak through me in a way that touches the people of Houston.

Something wonderful is to come.

"Go, therefore, and make disciples of all nations, baptizing them in the name of the Father and of the Son and of the Holy Spirit," - Matthew 28:19 HCSB

My Week in Houston, Part 1- June 17, 2018

This past week, I had the opportunity to serve in Houston, Texas to help with the rebuilding process. It was an incredible week. I got to meet wonderful homeowners, and great volunteers from all over the country. As the week went by, I noticed something with every story I would hear.

With each homeowner I would talk to, their stories all had the same theme: even in the hardest times in our lives, God is still good. That was so empowering to me. These people lost so much with Hurricane Harvey, but they continue to praise God.

It doesn't end there. The homeowners, my book of choice I packed for the trip, and the volunteers I spoke with all came back to that: in our darkest days, God is still in control.

I think about the poem "Footprints," where the man asks God why there was only one set of footprints in his darkest times of his life. He didn't understand why God would leave him. God replied, "in those times, it was I who carried you."

I have no doubt God put me in Texas for elite reason last week. I truly believe he needed to remind me of the fact that even in the darkest days, God is still good. I have seen my fair share of darkest days. Today would've been mine and Justin's first wedding anniversary. I often wonder what life would be like if he were still here, but it's so great to know that I can rest on the fact that he is rejoicing in heaven and is not in pain.

Even in our darkest days, God is still there. He is in control, and He is there to carry us when we need Him most.

My Week in Houston, Part 2- June 24, 2018

As I mentioned last week, I went to Houston to serve on a mission trip helping people rebuild their homes damaged by Hurricane Harvey last year. It was an amazing week for many reasons. For those who don't know, I love these types of mission trips, because I am able to learn all sorts of construction lessons! My passion for this actually started seven years ago.

When I was a freshman in college, I signed up to go to New Orleans to help rebuild homes damaged by Hurricane Katrina. I enjoyed it so much, I signed up to go three consecutive years after. In fact, it was through these trips to New Orleans Justin and I got to know each other!

After he died, I knew I wanted to participate more on mission trips. I wanted to do more with my time. So, I chose to go to Houston.

In preparing for this trip, I was telling myself not to set expectations, as I have learned on previous mission trips that this can affect my experiences and actions. But, naturally, expectations happen!

I remember riding up to the job site on the first day and thinking to myself how nice the neighborhood looked! Most of the homes were all brick, two stories, and seemed near perfect on the outside. I soon noticed that the inside of the homes were damaged.

I parallel this with many peoples' lives: things can look perfect to others on the outside, but on the inside, we can be an absolute wreck. We never know what kinds of burdens and challenges others are facing in the inside. This association spoke strongly to me.

I also learned some surprising statistics. The city of Houston is much larger than I realized, housing over 2 million people. After the devastation from Hurricane Harvey in August 2017, over 600,000 cars were destroyed, and over 400,000 homes were either damaged or destroyed. Do you know how many homes will be rebuilt this year from all of the known volunteer organizations in Houston? Only about 2,000.

This city still needs help. It may look like they've fully recovered on the outside looking in, but the city of Houston is still rebuilding, and need all the help they can get.

Ways to help:

1) Pray. Pray that volunteers will come as serve in the city of Houston.

2) Serve. Bring a church group, family, or hop on a plane yourself (this is what I did!) and go get your hands dirty! Talk with homeowners. Pray with strangers. Go serve in Houston.

3) Give. This doesn't even have to be monetary. Give your time. Give tools you don't need. Just give.

If you are interested in serving in Houston for a week or so, let me know! I can give you some resources to help you along the way. And remember: just because things look great on the outside does not mean things are great on the inside. Be present for those who need it.

"And whatever you do, in word or in deed, do everything in the name of the Lord Jesus, giving thanks to God the Father through Him." - Colossians 3:17 HCSB

Just a Widow- July 1, 2018

After Justin died, I found myself struggling to find my identity. Part of me felt like the old Stacie: the Stacie that had a loving husband.

Part of me felt broken, destroyed, and helpless. I really struggled finding my identity after Justin died. I realized then when I lost Justin, I lost more than just a husband. I lost my best friend, my confidant, my shoulder to cry on, my security, my adventure buddy, and so much more.

I discovered that when I wanted to go out and do something, I didn't have Justin here joining me. When I feel like cooking a new meal, Justin isn't here to try it and say how much he loves it (even if I burn it on accident). Justin was a big part of my identity: he was my husband, and I was his wife.

Now, I'm his widow.

Talk about a 180. When the term "widow" became part of my identity, I was so confused about the person I was.

That's when I realized: I may be a widow, but that's not my identity. So what is my identity?

Here's what I've come up with so far:

I'm a Christian, friend, daughter, and a counselor, to name a few. I am also compassionate, patient, sometimes stubborn, non-confrontational, and kind to others.

I believe in showing others a Christ-like love in all that I do. I believe that a small ripple of kindness can cause a big wave.

I'm still learning to enjoy activities without my husband by my side. It's a process, and it doesn't happen overnight. But, to think about where I was just seven months ago and where I am now, I would say I am making pretty good progress.

If you've recently lost someone special in your life, remember everything you are and everything you have. Don't label yourself as "just a widow."

You're so much more than that.

"Dear friends, let us love one another, because love is from God, and everyone who loves has been born of God and knows God." - 1 John 4:7 HCSB

Life after Loss- July 8, 2018

Life after loss is confusing.

It is a constant struggle to try to move forward, when all you want is the past.

But, this is not how life works.

When you lose someone special to you, it is so hard to keep moving forward. Ultimately, in your own time and way, you discover that you must continue on, while still remembering the person you lost.

For me, I am still trying to figure out my life after loss.

As far as what my future holds, I have no clue. None of us do. But, there are some things I have learned about life after loss:

1) Life is short

Losing Justin made me realize just how short life is. For him to be healthy one day and in a coma the next, it made me realize that I don't have time to waste another minute of the life I've been given. I am taking better care of myself, and I have taken it upon myself to travel more and experience some of God's greatest creations.

2) Love vs Loss

Have you ever heard the saying, "it's better to have loved and lost than to never have loved at all?" Well, it's 100% true, in my opinion. Even though I lost my husband five months after we got married, I'm so incredibly thankful I got to be the one he loved. I'm so grateful I got to be Mrs. Justin Baker. I'm so glad I got the chance to love him back. Even though he is no longer here, no amount of grief can take that kind of love away from me.

3) God is always with you.

It is sometimes hard to believe this, trust me. This was a lesson I had to learn the hard way. How could God be with me while letting my husband die so young?

The truth is, He was with me. He comforted me in my darkest nights. He gave me strength when I couldn't find any of my own. He continues to be by my side as the months have gone by. God may take us through trenches and trials, but He never leaves us there.

I'm learning new lessons every day. As I say often, it's a day by day journey. Sometimes, that's all we can do.

Bad Days – July 15, 2018

I remember the first few months after Justin's death, I would keep tabs on how I was doing mentally, emotionally, physically, and spiritually. I used this method to see how I was progressing in the grief process. I would feel encouraged when I would have a good week. I would feel like I was moving forward step by step.

Then I would have a bad day.

You know the kind: where you feel invincible one second, then the next you are ambushed with such a strong emotion that it knocks you down. These bad days were frustrating me for several different reasons: the biggest reason this bothered me so much was because it made me feel like I was moving backwards with my grief.

You see, my problem was that I was too focused on where I wanted to be and forgot to remind myself of where I used to be. The fact of the matter is I continue to grow and heal with each passing day.

Here is what I have learned about bad days. Just because you have a bad day doesn't mean you've taken a step backwards. It just means you've had a bad day: that's it. If I have a decent week, then have a bad day on the weekend from being so caught up in grief, it doesn't mean I'm not progressing. It just means I need to let my grief be grief for that moment (I'll dive more into this at a later time).

While these "bad days" in my grief don't happen as often or as intense as they used to, they still happen. I now know that when I have these bad days, I just need to roll with it and do what I need to do to make the best out of it, whether that be looking at old pictures, listening to music, or spending time in the Word.

Whatever you are going through, remember that a bad day is not a step backwards: it's just a bad day.

"Even in laughter a heart may be sad, and joy may end in grief." - Proverbs 14:13 HCSB

The Race – July 22, 2018

At the beginning of 2017, I set a New Year's resolution to run a 5k each month. From January to October, I was consistent: I was having so much fun crushing this goal, and my sweet Justin was there cheering me along the way at each race.

Then November came.

My race scheduled for November was the same week that we were in the hospital with Justin, living our worst nightmare.

I never raced in November. Or December.

In fact, as I've mentioned before, it took months for me to even try running at all. I was scared to run, as that's what Justin was doing when he went into cardiac arrest.

But, I was living in fear. And for me, living in fear wasn't living at all. So I started running again.

Fast forward to yesterday: I ran my first 5k since Justin died. Yesterday also marked eight months without Justin by my side. A mighty coincidence.

That race was tough, but I kept telling myself that I was tougher. The hills were hard to climb, but I've scaled mountains these last eight months. You see, when life hands us difficult circumstances we have two options: we can use those circumstances as an excuse to give up, or we can use those same circumstances as a reason to keep going.

It was strange not having Justin waiting to run the last half mile with me as he always did. I had to push myself this time, but I did it. It's been difficult, to say the least, not having my husband here with me these last eight months. But, I've made it this far.

Yesterday was a HUGE step forward for me, and I hope to continue the momentum.

And yes, I plan to finish the resolution I set for myself last year.

"Therefore, since we also have such a large cloud of witnesses surrounding us, let us lay aside every weight and the sin that so easily ensnares us. Let us run with endurance the race that lies before us," - Hebrews 12:1 HCSB

Letting Grief be Grief- July 29, 2018

What does grief look like?

In college, I learned about the stages of grief: denial, anger, bargaining, depression, and acceptance. When I lost my husband, I realized these stages of grief I learned some years ago were absolutely nothing like the grief I experienced.

Grief does not follow a concrete pattern, and no two victims of grief will have the same linear pattern.

So what does grief feel like?

For me, it's been a bunch of feelings in no particular order: anger, sadness, confusion, disorientation, regret, guilt... to name a few.

However, I've also experienced a deeper appreciation for life, and gratitude: gratitude for getting to be Justin's wife (albeit for just five months).

Some days I feel like crap. Some days I've been completely emotionally numb. Some days I flash back to November 2017. But some days I remember our wedding in June 2017. Some days I remember when Justin and I would play Mario Kart on his old Nintendo 64.

Reflection.

I reflect on what a gift God gave me for three and a half years. I reflect on how far I've come these past eight months.

No one can take that away from me.

So what's grief like? It just depends. Maybe bubble baths help you feel better. Perhaps watching old home movies or looking at old photos is what you need in order to grieve. Just let your grief be your grief- don't let someone tell you how to grieve, how long to grieve, or where to bottle up your grief. Do what you need to do to grieve, and when you're ready, take your first step forward.

Bitter or Better – August 5, 2018

It is so EASY to become bitter when bad things happen.

Since Justin's death, I have definitely had moments where I've allowed the bitterness to enter my heart. I couldn't help but feel bitter when I would see a random couple walk by holding hands. Things just weren't fair, in my eyes.

I've been doing a LOT of reflection on these *nearly* nine months without Justin, and the majority of my reflecting has been done this past month. Have I become bitter? Or have I become better?

Here's what I've decided: yeah, there's been times I've been bitter. I've been jealous of complete strangers looking so happy in public. But I've grown in ways, too.

Yeah, there have been times where bitterness has consumed me, but these past eight months have made me stronger. I've become closer to God, and that's a relationship that will never disappear from my life. I've learned to appreciate each day, and not take it for granted. I've become better.

I've said it before and I'll say it again: we were not created to constantly live in a state of grief. Yeah, I obviously miss Justin. Yeah, I've had moments of bitterness in my heart. But through all that has happened, I truly feel it has made me better in many different ways. I appreciate the gift of life so much more, and I cherish the people in it- even those random happy couples walking by.

When life gets rough, you can choose to be bitter (which is often the easiest route), OR you can choose to be better for it. Allow yourself to grow from the experiences that knock you down. Let yourself rise from the ashes of the fire that sent your world crumbling. If you come out stronger through those valleys in life, there's no doubt you will be better for it.

Extinguishing Expectations – August 12, 2018

"Will they be upset?"

"Will they be surprised?"

"Will they understand?"

It is so easy to get caught up in what others expect of us. In fact, it can consume us. So why is it so hard to stay away from this mindset?

I know the last several months, I have gotten too preoccupied with what people think of me. I have asked myself why this comes so naturally, but I haven't come up with any groundbreaking answers.

This mindset can be so damaging to how we choose to live our lives. We focus too much on what people expect us to do with our lives, and it helps no one.

The truth is, the less time we spend focusing on what others think of us, the more time we have to spend with family, friends, and for my life, spending more time in God's word. This is a lesson I'm slowly learning with each day.

I am reminding myself constantly that instead of getting caught up with wondering what people expect of me, I will choose to remember what I expect of myself. And you know something? I'm so much happier because of it. I don't worry about what others expect of me, and I am completely fine with that.

Extinguishing Expectations: Part 2 – August 19, 2018

Last week I talked about ridding our lives of the expectations others had on us. And honestly, that's where I planned to stop- I didn't expect a second part to this, but I couldn't ignore it. Last week, I listened to a sermon that talked about expectations, and I knew I needed to continue on this topic. This week, I'm going one step further.

While I was sitting at church last week, I realized I addressed releasing the grip on expectations others place on us, but I failed to mention the expectations we place on God many of us are guilty– we expect a blessed life if we live a good life. We expect a good job. We expect a happy family. We expect a nice house. We expect a marriage to last a lifetime.

At least, I know I did. I expected all of these things to just happen, as if it was guaranteed. I didn't expect Justin to go into cardiac arrest. I didn't expect to drive around the city in the dark for two hours, praying we would find him safe in a ditch somewhere. I didn't expect to find him listed as a John Doe at the hospital, lying there unconscious. I didn't expect him to die a week later. I didn't expect to become a widow when I was 25.

But this all happened.

We don't always get the life we expect, but that doesn't mean we should blame God. God doesn't promise that we will live a good and easy life. God doesn't promise we make it through without hitting rock bottom. The good news? He does promise He will be there to pick us up when we fall, if we let Him.

I've said it many times, but there is absolutely no way I've made it this far without God picking me up and carrying me at times. I didn't get the house full of kids, or the 60 year marriage I expected to have with Justin, but I had five AMAZING months of marriage to Justin. I had a husband who lived his life glorifying God. I was married to a man who put everyone else before himself, and loved me for me. Furthermore? I have the love of a Heavenly Father who will never leave me- I know this firsthand.

Life does not always go as we expect it to, but it is so important to remind ourselves that we are not alone when we are tossed into the trenches. Whether we are dealing with illness, tragedy, divorce, money problems, issues at work, marriage problems, WHATEVER it may be, God is there ready to catch us when we fall, and that we can be sure of. THAT we can expect.

Trust me on this.

"Rejoice in hope; be patient in affliction; be persistent in prayer."
- Romans 12:12 HCSB

For "The One who Comes After" – August 26, 2018

Let me start off by saying in NO WAY am I ready to start a serious relationship yet. Got it? Good.

Now, with that said, I've been asked by several people if I think I'll ever meet someone new. I've also been praying and thinking a LOT about my future, and what it may entail. God has given me such strength since Justin's death, and I know without Him I would not be in this place. I loved that I got to be the one married to Justin, yet at the same time I hate that we had just five months of marriage together.

One thing I did learn: I LOVED being married. Getting to be in a relationship where both individuals are giving 100% is such an incredible feeling. I loved Justin with everything I had, and he did the same for me.

For the most part, I would say I have grown accustomed to living on my own, and I have done fairly well being on my own, considering the circumstances. However, I know there's a possibility I may one day remarry. Again, this is NOT something I want right away, for obvious reasons. I was widowed when I was just 25 years old, and I know I've got a long life ahead of me, God willing. With that in mind, there is a chance I will find a new relationship down the road.

So, for whoever God has planned for me later down that road, there are a few things I want to mention…

1. My First Husband will always be a Part of Me

Just because my husband is dead does not mean the memories died with him. In fact, it is the memories that have helped me feel like part of him stays with me. Justin will always be a part of me, no matter where life takes me. Whoever God has planned for me, if anyone, must be comfortable with me bringing up occasional stories of my first love.

2. I Won't Take Love for Granted

When you lose a spouse, especially decades sooner than antici-
pated, you learn not to take love for granted. Because we aren't
promised tomorrow, I know how important it is to love those around
you any chance you get. This includes friends and family– not just a
significant other! Since Justin's death I am making more of an effort to
spend more quality time with friends and family. I think sometimes
people fear widows because they're afraid of competing with the de-
ceased, but it's so far from the truth: for me I know what it's like for
the love of my life to be ripped away from me, so I am going to be more
involved, engaged, and invested in the relationships God places me in.

3. I Will Never Compare You to Him

My love for Justin can never be duplicated, but that doesn't mean
I can never love again. What Justin and I had was so incredibly special:
it was a gift from God. And, I also know that if God placed someone
else in my life one day, that relationship will be an entirely new and
different experience.

4. I Can Live without You

This one is hard to admit. I never thought I could live without Justin. In fact, the thought of life without him made me sick to my stomach
before I was forced to live without him. And I have found out that while
it is the hardest thing I have done, I can live without my husband. When
moving forward is the only option you have, you move forward: no
matter how fast or slow you go. And, while I hope to never be a widow
a second time, I know that I will be ok, because I have done it already.

I have no clue what God has planned for my future. And while I
may not know God's plan for my life, I do know He has already started
stitching my life's story together. It's just a matter of figuring out which
chapters are for me.

"For I know the plans I have for you" — this is the Lord's declaration — "plans for your welfare, not for disaster, to give you a future and a hope." - Jeremiah 29:11 HCSB

Doors – September 2, 2018

There have been some strange coincidences around my house lately, all pertaining to doors. First, my garage door stopped working. I am also in the process of stripping the paint off the garage door to give it a new splash of color. Then, I noticed that the frame on my back door has a small crack in it. It still works fine, but has started to make a creak when I open and shut it. All of this has happened within the last week.

Fast forward to this past Wednesday night.

I was finishing up a workout in the living room, and was close to walking into the kitchen. I stopped to pick up my water bottle before I made my way there. Then, out of nowhere, I hear a cabinet door shut. By itself.

There is significance to this cabinet door.

When Justin was alive, one of my biggest pet peeves was that he would leave all of the cabinet doors open after getting what he needed. I never got mad at him for it, but I always thought to myself, "how hard is it to close the cabinet??"

When I heard the cabinet door shut, I instantly remembered not closing it all the way earlier that evening. It was slightly ajar, so it didn't take much more than the AC kicking on to shut it completely. All those times wishing Justin would just close the cabinet doors, and I start to do the same thing!

Still, as soon as I heard that cabinet door shut I instantly thought of Justin. Then I thought about all of the door-related occurrences happening in my house currently. Coincidence?

We have all heard the saying, "when one door closes, another opens." My mind keeps coming to that phrase. The door to my life with Justin closed almost a year ago (it'll be a year in November). Through the grief, the sleepless nights, the stressful trials that followed his death, the fear of the unknown for my life as a widow, and the uncertainty behind every corner, I see that God has opened other doors for me along the way.

He has led me to a wonderful new church, where I am given several opportunities to grow in my walk with the Lord. He has allowed me to participate on a mission trip, where I hopped on a plane by myself (my longest solo trip ever) to go help rebuild houses in Texas for a week. He has given me the courage to fight for each day, and He has allowed me to document my grief in a way that has reached thousands all over the world.

I know the cabinet door closed on its own because of the way I left it open earlier that night, but I also believe that is just what I needed to remind myself of all the doors God has propped open for me these past nine and a half months. Which doors are He keeping open for you?

"I know your works. Because you have limited strength, have kept My word, and have not denied My name, look, I have placed before you an open door that no one is able to close." - Revelation 3:8 HCSB

I can remember when Justin died, I found it very difficult to leave the house. I didn't want to. I even joined a gym just to give myself a reason to leave the house and do something. And it worked, for a while.

There were several reasons why I didn't want to leave my house. One reason was because Justin and I always did things together, and now that wasn't an option. Now I was on my own. If I wanted to get groceries, I had to drive to the store. If I wanted to go for a walk, it was my own company I had for the walk. And forget about going to the movies. Yes, I have wonderful friends and family that would invite me places to get me out of the house, and while I am so thankful for them, it just wasn't the same. For a good while, I chose not to do a lot of things because I didn't want to be alone doing them.

A major part of widowhood is discovering who you are once your loved one has passed on. It's a total identity check, and it can be a difficult process, to put it lightly. Though Justin and I were only married for five months, we were together for nearly four years, so trying to discover who I was felt like an incredibly daunting task.

As time had passed, I've learned how much I am capable of on my own. I'm stronger than I ever expected to be. I'm learning to branch out, which has not been an easy task for this introvert widow.

When I was ready to start branching out and learn who I was/who I wanted to be, I asked myself: in what ways can I challenge myself? So, I started trying new things.

I'm learning to play guitar.

I'm playing in my first golf tournament next week.

I've started running 5ks again.

I have plans to travel to new places in the future.

I've hopped on a plane solo and flown to Texas to serve on a mission trip for a week.

I have become a fitness coach as a side gig.

And, if you didn't catch my most recent announcement, I'm beginning to write my very own book on grief, and plan to release it next fall.

Yes, I am branching out and challenging myself in new and wonderful ways, but you can too, and you don't have to wait to become widowed to do so.

I saw a quote the other day, and it went something like this:

Everyone has two lives: the life they have before they only realize they have one life, and after.

What does branching out mean to you? It could mean going out with that person you've had your eye on for a while. Perhaps it's meeting new people. Maybe you finally sign up for that class you've been wanting to take, or maybe branching out to you means you save up to finally go on the vacation of your dreams. The best part? You can branch out and do those things you've been wanting to do now. All it takes is that first step, and a little bit of faith.

"Brothers, do not grow weary in doing good." - 2 Thessalonians 3:13 HCSB

"Why did Justin have to die?"

"Why were we only married for five months?"

"Why do I have to be a widow?"

I have dealt with so many "whys" these past ten months. Many of which presented themselves early in the first few weeks. It is exhausting. There are no answers to these questions, but I would still ask them anyway.

Maybe in your life, you have been asking your own set of "whys:"

"Why did my marriage have to end?"

"Why don't I have children?"

"Why did my child have to die?"

"Why am I so unhappy at my job?"

What helped me with my "whys" was remembering the story of Job. He had so many good things in his life, and gave thanks to God for his blessings. So, when Satan took his children, his livestock, and his servants, he could have easily turned away from God. He could have easily become angry with God. Instead, he fell to the ground and worshiped God.

Wow.

Even Job's wife said to be angry at God for allowing such pain and tragedy, but Job didn't listen to her. He continued praising God. Even in mourning. And, because he continued praising God in the midst of tragedy after tragedy, God blessed him immensely.

I could keep asking those "whys" I mentioned earlier, but the truth is, knowing the answers doesn't bring Justin back. And at this point, I don't want to bring Justin back. He is free from pain and suffering in Heaven, and there's no way I'd ask that he come back to a world where pain is everywhere.

Whatever your "whys" may be, remember that God is in control. We all face tragedies and tribulations in life. Even as Christians. The good news? God will give you the strength to overcome your tragedies, but only if you allow him into your life to do so. That is the only way I've made it this far through my grief. So, whatever trials you're facing in life, give it to God and allow Him to carry you through the valleys.

Then Job stood up, tore his robe, and shaved his head. He fell to the ground and worshiped, saying: "Naked I came from my mother's womb, and naked I will leave this life. The Lord gives, and the Lord takes away. Praise the name of Yahweh. Throughout all this Job did not sin or blame God for anything." - Job 1:20-22

A Good Place – September 30, 2018

If there is one lesson I've learned it is that there is no cookie cutter concept of grief. There's no rule book, no timeline, no calendar of grief events.

Luckily, other people who have gone through grief have offered support and resources that helped them along the way, in hopes of helping others. I've read several books on grief, and each book has different concepts and different approaches on handling grief. These are created in attempts to help others who grieve, which is why I decided to write a book myself.

I have been focusing on the format of my book, and reflecting a LOT on all that has happened these past ten months. Upon reflecting, I have determined this:

I am in a good place.

I can recall the first days and weeks after Justin died, and I remember thinking to myself how my life would never be the same (which was true). I also believed I would never be happy again (which, thankfully, was not true).

This does not mean I don't have bad days. I still have times where grief just puts my mind in a fog, and I have trouble focusing on other things. But, all in all, I am in a good place. I have far better good days than bad. I smile and laugh and joke again. I crave living my life to the fullest.

This is the focus I want my book to take. No, there is no rule book for grief. I can't wave a magic wand to take the pain away, and neither can you. But, if you allow yourself time and have faith in the Lord that he will help guide you, you can find healing. You can find happiness. You can find a good place to be again. Don't give up on yourself.

Sorry – October 7, 2018

This post has been on my heart for a while, but I have been hesitant to write it, fearing it may be taken the wrong way. But, with everything that's happened the past year, caring what other people think is really at the bottom of my list, so here we go…

I don't want you to feel sorry for me.

Yeah, you read that right.

PLEASE hear me out. I loved Justin so much. We had so many plans for our future, and I absolutely hate that he was taken away from me so soon. I've had sleepless nights. I have had dreams where he came back to me. I've had nightmares where I lost him over and over again.

But, I don't want you to feel sorry for me, and here is why…

It's been almost a year since Justin died. While there have been many days where I didn't think I would make it without him, I did. While there have been times I didn't know what to do with my life, I figured things out on my own. There have been times of weakness, as well as times of strength. In my lowest points, I've had friends and family there to pick me back up again. Even though Justin is gone, I'm blessed in many ways.

So, don't feel sorry for me. My weakest point was losing Justin, but my strongest has come from learning and adapting to my new life without him. This experience has made me strong in many ways, and has helped and inspired hundreds of people.

God has this, so don't feel sorry for me.

"But he said to me, "My grace is sufficient for you, for my power is made perfect in weakness." Therefore I will boast all the more gladly about my weaknesses, so that Christ's power may rest on me." - 2 Corinthians 12:9 NIV

Limits – October 28, 2018

You have probably heard the Wayne Gretzky quote, "You miss 100% of the shots you don't take." Up until recently, I never thought much about that quote. I mean, it's nice, but it never has been something I lived by.

There have been instances in my life where I lived in fear: fear of failing, fear of falling, and fear of messing up. In the last year, those fears have become smaller. My biggest fear of losing my husband came true unexpectedly, and I was forced to face this fear of being a 25 year old widow without anyone asking my permission. My fears of failure and falling and messing up were temporarily forgotten, as I had more important matters to worry about.

When I announced my decision to write my book, those three fears slowly crept back into my life.

What if I fail as an author?

What if no one buys my book?

What if mess up my one chance? What's the point of trying?

I could easily let these fears keep me from pursuing this adventure. But recently, I came across this quote again.

You miss 100% of the shots you don't take.

You see, we could easily miss out on our biggest adventures in life out of pure fear of failing, so we don't even try. Instead, we need to stand up, look that fear in the eye, and push it aside.

I don't know what your dreams are, and I don't know what your fears are. But, I've learned one thing: I would rather try and fail than not try and forever regret letting my fear keep me hostage.

So, as I'm working on this book, and for every adventure to come, I'm not letting my fear limit my capability.

Don't let your fears limit you.

"I sought the Lord, and He answered me and delivered me from all my fears." - Psalms 34:4

Reflecting on a Year – November 14, 2018

I suppose that, to get a clearer picture of my life, I should tell you my story of how I became a widow. Justin and I were together for three years when we got married in June of 2017. I never thought I would find someone so loving to share my life with. He was kind, caring, loving, funny, and everything I had hoped for in a husband.

On November 14 of that same year, Justin went out for a run. He was training for the Boston Marathon, which he had qualified for just two months prior. I left work late that day, and tried calling Justin on my way home. It eventually went to voicemail. I thought to myself, "He must still be out running." I couldn't wait to get home to him that day. I was always happy to see Justin after we both got home from work, but for some reason, that day, I was so looking forward to one of his hugs.

When I got home, it was about two hours after he went out for a run and he wasn't home yet. Although he was a distance runner, I knew something was wrong. I immediately called his parents to see if he had finished his run at their house, which was just a few miles down the road. When they hadn't heard from him either, we started driving around town looking for Justin.

I was calling all of our friends that lived close by. No one had heard from Justin. Some even hopped in their own cars to aid in the search. I drove his usual running routes: no sign of him. For two hours, we drove in separate cars to cover as much ground as we could. We called both hospitals in the city and we called law enforcement. No one knew where Justin was.

About two hours into the search, Justin's mother called me to tell me that Justin was at the hospital. She worked with law enforcement and they eventually located him for us. The trouble that we ran into was that since Justin was running, he had no keys, no phone, and no identification on him, so he was in the hospital as a John Doe until we finally found him.

When we got to the hospital, they brought his parents and me into a consultation room, where two officers and a chaplain stood. At first, no one said a word. Then, the doctor came in and told us that Justin suffered from cardiac arrest while on his run, and collapsed less than a mile from the house. Thankfully, someone watched him go down, and called 911. They had to shock him multiple times, but eventually brought him back to life. However, he had gone without oxygen too long.

"So, he's alive?" I asked the doctor. It felt like they were taking an eternity to beat around the bush and tell us what happened. Finally, we got a "yes." In that moment, that was all that I needed.

They told us that he was still unconscious, and was not responding to stimuli. But, he was alive. They took him to ICU that night where they ran some tests. Justin had MRIs, CT scans, and tests I can't even recall. For a week, Justin stayed in the ICU. At times, we thought he would regain consciousness. He would even open his eyes at times. However, we found out that his eyes opening, his slight movements in his extremities, and his coughing were all involuntary movements. A week after being admitted into the hospital, we were told by doctors that Justin would forever be braindead. Nothing more could be done.

The hardest decision I have ever had to make was to take my husband of five months off of life support. I was so thankful to have so much support coming from my family, Justin's family, and all of our friends through that whole week. However, we all knew the life Justin had before, and we knew he would have made the choice we had to make for him. That entire week in the hospital was excruciating. The days that followed were excruciating. The weeks and months? Yep. You guess it.

Excruciating.

I am telling you all of this for a reason. I felt so many emotions throughout this valley. I was angry at God. I could not understand how

God could take someone so kind away from me so soon. Why did Justin have to be taken so soon?

It is so hard to know these answers. Most of the time, we never know the answers. And frankly, that sucks. But, it is my prayer that as you progress through my book, you can see that in the valleys, and the trenches, there can be joys that come from loss. Because there can be joy after grief. There can be peace after pain. If you allow it, there can be happiness after agony.

Conclusion

Time has passed since my sweet Justin died. I have learned many lessons. I have made new friends through the journey. I am convinced that no one can truly be an "expert" on grief, as it is different for each person. However, I feel like those who have experienced grief firsthand have an inside look at how life can crumble.

When Justin died, my life crumbled. My future plans crumbled. I am convinced a piece of my heart died when Justin took his last breath. I was broken in every sense of the word. During the first few months, I kept thinking to myself, "I hope my life can be normal again one day."

Well, I have learned that life will never be the way it was. My world changed the day I met Justin, and my world changed the day he died.

Still, as I have mentioned before, good days can come, even after the worst of days. I firmly believe that God is still good. He has used this story to reach thousands of people in multiple ways.

I say this to tell you that, no matter what days you are experiencing, and no matter what adversities you face, you can come back from this. You can stand again after falling.

You can come back from broken.

www.ingramcontent.com/pod-product-compliance
Lightning Source LLC
Chambersburg PA
CBHW031254280526
45784CB00004B/1853